IMMIGRANT CHRONICLE

Peter Skrzynecki was born in 1945 in Germany and came to Australia in 1949. He has published seventeen books of poetry and prose and won several literary prizes, including the Grace Leven Poetry Prize and the Henry Lawson Short Story Award. In 1989 he was awarded the Order of Cultural Merit by the Polish government, and in 2002 he received the Medal of the Order of Australia (OAM) for his contribution to multicultural literature. His memoir, *The Sparrow Garden*, was shortlisted for the National Biography Award. He is an adjunct associate professor in the School of Humanities and Languages at the University of Western Sydney.

By the same author:

Joseph's Coat: An Anthology of Multicultural Writing (editor)
The Wild Dogs (short stories)
The Beloved Mountain (novel)
Night Swim (poetry)
Rock'n'Roll Heroes (short stories)
Easter Sunday (poetry)
The Cry of the Goldfinch (novel)
Influence: Australian Voices (editor)
Time's Revenge (poetry)
The Sparrow Garden (memoir)
Old/New World: New and Selected Poems (poetry)
Boys of Summer (novel)

IMMIGRANT CHRONICLE

Peter Skrzynecki

UQP

First published 1975 by University of Queensland Press
PO Box 6042, St Lucia, Queensland 4067 Australia
Reprinted 1991, 1992, 1993, 1994
This edition 2002
Reprinted 2003, 2004 (twice), 2005, 2006, 2007, 2008, 2009,
2010, 2011, 2012, 2013, 2015

www.uqp.com.au

© Peter Skrzynecki

This book is copyright. Except for private study, research,
criticism or reviews, as permitted under the Copyright Act,
no part of this book may be reproduced, stored in a retrieval system,
or transmitted in any form or by any means without prior
written permission. Enquiries should be made to the publisher.

Typeset by University of Queensland Press
Printed in Australia by McPherson's Printing Group

Cataloguing in Publication Data
National Library of Australia

Skrzynecki, Peter, 1945- .
  Immigrant chronicle/by Peter Skrzynecki.

  I. Title. (Series UQP poetry)

A821.3

ISBN 978 0 7022 3387 6

for Brian Couch and Tony Garnett

I stare
At the photograph
And refuse to answer
The voices
Of red gables
And a cloudless sky.

On the river's bank
A lone tree
Whispers:
"We will meet
Before you die."

Contents

Immigrants at Central Station, 1951

It was sad to hear
The train's whistle this morning
At the railway station.
All night it had rained.
The air was crowded
With a dampness that slowly
Sank into our thoughts —
But we ate it all:
The silence, the cold, the benevolence
Of empty streets.

Time waited anxiously with us
Behind upturned collars
And space hemmed us
Against each other
Like cattle bought for slaughter.

Families stood
With blankets and packed cases —
Keeping children by their sides,
Watching pigeons
That watched them.

But it was sad to hear
The train's whistle so suddenly —
To the right of our shoulders
Like a word of command.
The signal at the platform's end
Turned red and dropped
Like a guillotine —
Cutting us off from the space of eyesight

While time ran ahead
Along glistening tracks of steel.

1

Feliks Skrzynecki

My gentle father
Kept pace only with the Joneses
Of his own mind's making —
Loved his garden like an only child,
Spent years walking its perimeter
From sunrise to sleep.
Alert, brisk and silent,
He swept its paths
Ten times around the world.

Hands darkened
From cement, fingers with cracks
Like the sods he broke,
I often wondered how he existed
On five or six hours' sleep each night —
Why his arms didn't fall off
From the soil he turned
And tobacco he rolled.

His Polish friends
Always shook hands too violently,
I thought . . . *Feliks Skrzynecki,*
That formal address
I never got used to.
Talking, they reminisced
About farms where paddocks flowered
With corn and wheat,
Horses they bred, pigs
They were skilled in slaughtering.
Five years of forced labour in Germany
Did not dull the softness of his blue eyes.

I never once heard
Him complain of work, the weather
Or pain. When twice
They dug cancer out of his foot,
His comment was: "but I'm alive".

Growing older, I
Remember words he taught me,
Remnants of a language
I inherited unknowingly —
The curse that damned
A crew-cut, grey-haired
Department clerk
Who asked me in dancing-bear grunts:
"Did your father ever attempt to learn English?"

On the back steps of his house,
Bordered by golden cypress,
Lawns — geraniums younger
Than both parents,
My father sits out the evening
With his dog, smoking,
Watching stars and street lights come on,
Happy as I have never been.

At thirteen,
Stumbling over tenses in Caesar's *Gallic War,*
I forgot my first Polish word.
He repeated it so I never forgot.
After that, like a dumb prophet,
Watched me pegging my tents
Further and further south of Hadrian's Wall.

Heirlooms

for David Evans

The wind turns
A page of my primer
And speaks in a language
More recognizable
Than Old English —
Bends the gums and pines outside
With the sound of rain
And snow in the mountains.

Alone, I sit at a table
While my family sleeps
And rooms stir
Against the arms of winter.
The clock marks time
At 2 a.m. —
Shrugs its shoulders
At the suggestion
Of slowing down.

"At your table
And on such a night?
Why, and for whom?"

The wind replies
Across a page of Charms —
And I remember hearing voices
A long time ago
That made promises
At a cradle and tomb.

Aurea mediocritas

A wire divides
The clouds and grass.
You place a finger
On the rust of a barb —

Hold your breath
As catfish rise,
Turning from the shallows
Of roots and slime.

A blood-bird settles
In the arms of a vine —
Blots out the sun
With a turn of its head.

The midday heat
Encircles your eyes —
Blurs the scenery
That mountains enclose.

Children climb
The banks of a creek —
Showering the water
With pebbles and leaves.

Plovers silently
Rise from a sand-bar:
Fly down a track
Where cattle pass.

You place a finger
On the rust of a barb.
A wire divides
The clouds and grass.

St Patrick's College

Impressed by the uniforms
Of her employer's sons,
Mother enrolled me at St Pat's
With never a thought
To fees and expenses — wanting only
"What was best".

From the roof
Of the secondary school block
Our Lady watched
With outstretched arms,
Her face overshadowed by clouds.
Mother crossed herself
As she left me at the office —
Said a prayer
For my future intentions.
Under the principal's window
I stuck pine needles
Into the motto
On my breast:
Luceat Lux Vestra
I thought was a brand of soap.

For eight years
I walked Strathfield's paths and streets,
Played chasings up and down
The station's ten ramps —
Caught the 414 bus
Like a foreign tourist,
Uncertain of my destination
Every time I got off.

For eight years
I carried the blue, black and gold
I'd been privileged to wear:
Learnt my conjugations
And Christian decorums for homework,
Was never too bright at science
But good at spelling;
Could say The Lord's Prayer
In Latin, all in one breath.

My last day there
Mass was offered up
For our departing intentions,
Our Lady still watching
Above, unchanged by eight years' weather.
With closed eyes
I fervently counted
The seventy-eight pages
Of my *Venite Adoremus,*
Saw equations I never understood
Rubbed off the blackboard,
Voices at bus stops, litanies and hymns
Taking the right-hand turn
Out of Edgar Street for good;
Prayed that Mother would someday be pleased
With what she'd got for her money —
That the darkness around me
Wasn't "for the best"
Before I let my light shine.

Ancestors

Who are these shadows
That hang over you in a dream —
The bearded, faceless men
Standing shoulder to shoulder?

What secrets
Do they whisper into the darkness —
Why do their eyes
Never close?

Where do they point to
From the circle around you —
To what star
Do their footprints lead?

Behind them are
Mountains, the sound of a river,
A moonlit plain
Of grasses and sand.

Why do they
Never speak — how long
Is their wait to be?

Why do you wake
As their faces become clearer —
Your tongue dry
As caked mud?

From across the plain
Where sand and grasses never stir
The wind tastes of blood.

Elegy for Don McLaughlin

An only child also
You were equally spoilt —
Taken to both extremes,
Paradise and Inferno;
While parents kept guard
With upraised hands
Against vices and year-round chills.

Your voice
A good-luck charm
You sang like Burns wrote poetry —
Purely, the accent on love;
At concerts and plays
It drew admiration
As death draws silence.

We raced each other
To school in the mornings;
Beginning at opposite ends of the hill
On which St Peter's stands,
Swerving and skiting
On our bikes — unafraid
Of cars or Sister Brendan's cautions,
Laughing, out of breath.
Two fifth grade heroes
Chastized before the class –
Called "bold, brazen lads"
For the nth time.

On Berala station
They told me how you died —
With all the "ifs" and "buts"
That make Fate
So ominous and unkind:
A stolen car, the head-on smash,
You the only one
Not to survive.
A girl in a yellow dress
Held a transistor
To the wind:
              the Stones
Thumped out *The Last Time*
As our train
Came noisily in.

I wondered
How dark the night had been,
If any song
Had come to mind?

In those morning runs
You always beat me up the hill.
Younger by two years
I was fifteen when you died —
Old enough for self-esteem
And showing I wouldn't cry.
Now, on the same road,
I catch up to you
Without even having to try.

A part of the air I breathe

for Judith

1. Conception

At last
You have come — into the night
And fog that blankets
Our house:
Like an expected visitor
That failed to arrive
At a promised time.

We stop
Looking at clocks —
Keep on tearing off
Months from
A calendar.

Somewhere
In your fluid darkness
You have become
A part of the air
I breathe —
Of the sunlight
You will never grasp:
The dreams
That will confound you
Like a jig-saw puzzle
That always has
A missing piece.

Already
There is a weight
Upon your unformed shoulders —
The pull and grind
Of ancient tides.

The world
Is waiting like
A fairytale witch —
Her hand
Dipped in a bag
Full of bones
And gold pieces.

2. Night call

Awakened by
Your cries
We stumble
From our dreams —

One, two
Or three times a night,
Lost for direction
As we tread the darkness
Towards you,

Not knowing
Whether pain or hunger
Has opened
Your eyes to the cold.

Even
Without light
You know us
By our voices —

The touch
And warmth of hands:
By echoes
That carry
Like a message
Through the house.

In my arms
You turn
Like a shy, hooded animal
Burrowing
Into the ground —

Frantic, trembling,
As if a net
Dragged
At your heels:

Thursday's child —
Born in autumn
Out of mist and rain,
Far to go
And one life
To get there —

But surviving, so far,
And now winter
In the making.

How far
Will you go from us
Before learning
Of dreams
More bitter
Than the waking?

3. *Before her*

Across the yard
Pencil-pines cast afternoon shadows —
Form the crossed peaks
Of a valley where
A child is taking her first steps.

A dragonfly darts
Over the child's head —
Hovers above a pond.
Fish nibble at roots
Of floating ribbon-grass.

She is reaching for a branch —
For the sky and ground:
Falling and standing,
Laughing as she rolls.

The morning's rain
Still hangs in the air.
Clouds darken the western horizon.
She turns at the sound
Of cars and houses —
The gate she cannot open.

Peering into the abyss
That someday will be there,
She hesitates
At the edge of a shadow —
Looks up, startled, unafraid:
Ignorant of my presence
And the silent meanings of love and sorrow.

Evening and light descend.
Summer is finished tomorrow.

4. Eleven months old

Rain has settled
Into your life once more —
The long chills of morning
And the dampness of night
That brought you into
The world last winter.

No longer are we
Strangers to each other:
Both have learnt
The meaning of smiles —
How to listen for sounds
From behind a closed door.

Both have lived
Through four seasons
That will mostly be forgotten —
Have worn a separate path
Over unfenced allotments
Of pain and joy.

Having taken
Your first steps
The world is no longer so wide.
Something in your life
Is waiting to be set free.
Something else has died.

10 Mary Street

For nineteen years
We departed
Each morning, shut the house
Like a well-oiled lock,
Hid the key
Under a rusty bucket:
To school and work —
Over that still too-narrow bridge,
Around the factory
That was always burning down.

Back at 5p.m.
From the polite hum-drum
Of washing clothes
And laying sewerage pipes,
My parents watered
Plants — grew potatoes
And rows of sweet corn:
Tended roses and camellias
Like adopted children.
Home from school earlier
I'd ravage the backyard garden
Like a hungry bird —
Until, bursting at the seams
Of my little blue
St Patrick's College cap,
I'd swear to stay off
Strawberries and peas forever.

The house stands
In its china-blue coat —
With paint guaranteed
For another ten years.
Lawns grow across
Dug-up beds of
Spinach, carrots and tomato.
(The whole block
Has been gazetted for industry).

For nineteen years
We lived together —
Kept pre-war Europe alive
With photographs and letters,
Heated discussions
And embracing gestures:
Visitors that ate
Kielbasa, salt herrings
And rye bread, drank
Raw vodka or cherry brandy
And smoked like
A dozen Puffing Billies.

Naturalized more
Than a decade ago
We became citizens of the soil
That was feeding us —
Inheritors of a key
That'll open no house
When this one is pulled down.

Devil fish

A rat-trap mouth, skinless,
Each bone a grasshopper's leg —
Eyes like portholes we can't look into
From anywhere on zones of palm or ice.

Avoiding sun, catgut and nets to entice,
It swims under heaven's feet and ours.

Rising from blacked-out caverns of green foam,
Leopard-spotted like bullet holes;
Ignorant of storms washed up in cowrie shells
It survives an arc of rainbows and flying fish.

Dumb with purpose
It wanders the floor of a lantern world:
Celluloid eyes rolling in a head
That is a bone of compasses, hinged to all direction.

A side-on profile is the kneeling angel,
Streamlined by tail fins — folded small wings
In prayer,
                    but never to watch stars burning like coals
Above pits of darkness we shall never climb.

Exiled from a pock-marked sun
It follows its namesake from host to host
While prey falls like manna through a bottomless jaw.

Cattle

With their boxing-glove muzzles
They will stand in your path, heads lowered,
Or run stumbling through bracken
And creeks for no reason,
The grass alive with their fear.

Their bodies heavy
With milk and beef — awkward
As felled timber, they live
Herded by dogs and whips,
By our curses and impatience.

In downpours and mists
They stand like mute sentinels — immobile
With solemn, wide-open eyes,
Staring through hills and fences.

At night they bellow
Across paddocks and gullies,
Wake us from sleep and reassure us
Of our dreams and homestead.

Branded with fire
They have plodded through
Grass, mud and water for centuries —
Leaving, across continents,
A cleft print

That man will decipher
As an omen of his final hunger.

Carpe diem

Among the rainflowers
Robins sing at first light —
In patches of mist
That hang over a garden:

Yellowbreasts and greyheads
Perched sideways on stems —
Piping to each other,
At play on foxgloves and lupins.

A wagtail swoops down
From the roadside gums —
Watches sparrows feed
On grain that was spilt.

Cows have gathered
Under a mulberry tree —
Silently wait for
Someone to come out.

A woman will walk
Through the garden,
Bucket and stool in hand —
Be met by a pair of dogs:

She will bypass
Robins, wagtail and sparrows —
Walk down a track
That sunrise later follows.

Stopping overnight at Mile Ridge

A honeyeater sways
On the rim of a flower —
Black and white
Against yellow and red.

Last night she told us
How the birds
Return in spring —
Live in her orchards
And wildflower garden.

"You know what
The season will be like
By their songs —
As if they anticipate
Floods or a drought.

"What are homesteads
And gardens for —
If not to house friends
And passing ghosts?"

On a white-washed veranda
The woman stops talking,
Her face in shadow
Under a straw-brimmed hat.
"Anyway, why harm the small birds?"

A honeyeater sways
On the rim of a flower —
Pauses, on trembling wings,
Listening to her words.

The birth of a son

for Andrew

"The birth of a son
Should prompt you to write a poem,"
A friend told me
Last month over the phone.

I sat and thought,
Read a newspaper —
Walked around the house alone,
Picked dead leaves
Off the umbrella-tree.
Still no poem came.

The baby cried
And the house grew larger
With clothes and pram,
Toys, bunny-rugs — headaches
That arrived without notice
(Doors and windows were left open
But they were always
Reluctant to go).

Still no poem.
Only at night the sound
Of breathing
             and footsteps
That are still to come —
Hands that have no weight to carry
Across a threshold
He already owns.

I think of my father
And the house he lives in —
The land that I came from
And have never known.
My friend's suggestion strikes
Like sharpened stones
At night in the darkness

When I speak to my bones.

Elegy for Michael Dransfield

1

Not even
A crowd of slaters at your elbow
To intone a requiem
For the death of light —
Snail, cricket, earthworm
To move aside
For a hearse that passes on.

2

Behind the cat-eyed slit
Of disbelief
And the pumpkin-round stare
Of admiration
Only the bravest had nothing to say —
The most knowledgeable
Stood beside mirrors and each other
Conversing with Christ
About the dangers of being remembered
Too much after death.

But remembrance gathers
Like a flock of geese, triumphant
Above the naked wires
That bind this earth to its corners —
Rises above backyard lanes
Of bricks and rotting crates:
Incensed suites where gods and queens
Spawn their progenies
In the night by perspex lampshades
And footsteps run
Through a house where no one
Lives or knocks on doors.

3

Corpses of ants
And splinters of glass
Illuminate the one great epitaph to bury you
And all men forever —
Poet, fish, mouse or sparrow
Without cross or marble headstone.

4

Even prophets
Of eternity wear *Hic Jacet*
As a headband, pause
At the abyss of cracked memories
And the Hellespont
That runs between unfinished words:
Wear epitaphs of the same cloth
As tree leaf, flower, pebble —
Or Death, that stands
By traffic lights and plaza windows,
Hands in pockets, shoulders hunched,
Staring randomly at eyes
That blink and hurry past —
Or that guileless wanderer Instinct
Who pipes his ballads
So that children and insects follow.

Pelicans Coorong

after the lithograph by John Olsen

With their saucepan-like bellies
And candlestick necks
They inhabit a landscape
That rolls forward
From a hill.

One is watching
Suspiciously, with a look
That refuses
To answer questions —
Squats, almost aloof,
Feeding a headless fish
To its young.

Another lands
With outspread feet —
Straddles half the horizon
With the sun
At its eye:
                        the movement of webs
Arrested
                like
A shuffling of cards
In mid-air.

Front-on, their beaks
Point earthward
Like the blades of a knife —
Through heat
And silence, the glare
Of eroded hills:

Below the water of their timid eyes
That reflects The Darkness
From which hands
Arise.

Diamond snake

Taken from your keeper's bag
You lie coiled along my arm,
Tongue flicking at a kerosene lamp
And moths that night released.

He tells me you are harmless.
Nodding, I disbelieve.

The crack of a branch
And you turn at the moon — stabbing
The darkness I cannot touch.
My arm caressed by a stream of iced water
I wait for you to fall off.

To forget you I look
At the ground — piling shreds
Of leaves on to a piece of glass.
The men have stopped dealing cards.
Night has camped itself around us.

With you staring away from me
I turn towards the hut,
Watching, from the corner of my eyes
Your skin:
                and a thousand tiny fires
Burning in the prisms of your scales.

Gleaming like a scythe
You sweep and cut through shadows of grass.
Each time, face-on,
I see your eyes like stains of water
On the page of a book
I must find and read.

Cancer

Why should I look
Into mirrors and glass surfaces —
Try to see a face
That no longer is there?

Enough that my fingers
Can find a vein:
That my eyes
Can open and close.

Day and night
Pain moves up and down
My spine — like water
Seeking its level.

What comfort
Is there for me in acceptance —
Having come face to face
With God and the devil?

Insomnia

At first a taste
Of salt in your mouth — sticky,
Like rubber half-melted.

In the darkness
Of blankets your fingers
Grow numb, open Bibles and throw fish scraps
To appease the scavenger birds
Announcing dawn.

Hand scoop hollows
Into the mattress — look for warm sands
And the incoming tide.
You find bones, seaweed,
Rusted iron that cuts your wrists like teeth.

It was to have been
A pilgrim's journey. You prayed
For strong winds and fair weather,
A current to bear you
Within the sight of landfall.

Christ awaited you
At Emmaus, in the shade
Of limestone caves and willows.

Dead parents could not
Have broken through with pleas
To your waxen eyes
Under a starfish garden.

Light pierces the curtains,
Floods the shorelines between
Door and bed — widening, deepening,
Covering the floor.

Along the inlet
Where fresh water meets the night's tide
Bloodsuckers move
In dark weeds.

Crossing the Red Sea

1

Many slept on deck
Because of the day's heat
Or to watch a sunset
They would never see again —
Stretched out on blankets and pillows
Against cabins and rails:
Shirtless, in shorts, barefooted,
Themselves a landscape
Of milk-white flesh
On a scoured and polished deck.

Voices left their caves
And silence fell from its shackles,
Memories strayed
From behind sunken eyes
To look for shorelines —
Peaks of mountains and green rivers
That shared their secrets
With storms and exiles.

2

1949, and the war
Now four years dead —
Neither masters nor slaves
As we crossed a sea
And looked at red banners
That Time was hoisting
In mock salute.

3

Patches and shreds
Of dialogue
Hung from fingertips
And unshaven faces —
Offering themselves
As a respite
From the interruption
Of passing waves.

"I remember a field
Of red poppies, once behind the forest
When the full moon rose."

"Blood
Leaves similar dark stains —
When it runs for a long time
On stones or rusted iron."

(And the sea's breath
Touched the eyes
Of another Lazarus
Who was saying a prayer
In thanksgiving
For miracles)

4

All night
The kindness
Of the sea continued —
Breaking into
Walled-up griefs
That men had sworn
Would never be disclosed,
Accepting outflung denunciations
With a calmness
That brought a reminder
Of people listening to requiems,
Pine trees whispering
Against a stone wall in the breeze;
Or a trembling voice
That sang at the rails
When the ship first sailed
From the sorrow
Of northern wars.

5

Daybreak took away
The magic of dreams,
Fragments of apparitions
That became
More tangible than words —
Echoes and reflections
Of the trust
That men had bartered
For silence.

Had we talked
Of death
Perhaps something
More than time
Would have been lost.

But the gestures
Of darkness and starlight
Kept our minds
Away from the finalities
Of surrender —
As they beckoned towards
A blood-rimmed horizon
Beyond whose waters
The Equator
Was still to be crossed.

Death mask

Hands were
Never so tender — so hesitant,
As when touching the skin
Of a dead man.

You almost
Felt like speaking — knowing
Everything you said
Took your mind
Away from the closed eyes.

Water moved
Over your fingers
Like a drug — the cold heaviness
Of plaster falling
Out of your hands itself.

Never once
Did you step back — survey
Your work
And look for perspectives.

When it was over
You noticed how easily
The head moved — from side to side,
Almost obediently:

As if grateful
For the time you were giving
To the dead —
With a tenderness
You would
To a new-born child.

Leaving home

My first country appointment
Was the last thing we expected —
Three of us, caught unaware
By ignorance and faith:
Our dull-witted, frog-mouthed obedience
To the letter of the law.

Counting door handles, ringing telephones
And office boys with denture smiles,
I waited three hours
For a two-minute interview;
Watching myself outside in the rain,
My severed head under one arm,
Body upright — best white shirt and tie —
A black suit to outdo
The Pallbearer of the Year!
A red-and-white sign at my feet:
"Cabbages for Sale."
The fiddler from Chagall's village
Was inviting me to dance.

The man behind the desk
Never once looked me in the eyes —
His face the back of my application papers.
Hawk-nosed, crew-cut, with
A *Tally-Ho* paper skin,
He was the millionth person
That couldn't pronounce my name.
No more, no less,
The verdict came next day by phone:
"You must go."

We packed the car
Like a war-time train — clothes,
Books, records, the poems
I'd started writing;
Said goodbye so quickly
I forgot for a moment where I was going.

Three hundred miles
Up the New England Highway, I stopped;
Unloaded my bags for the night;
Swore that Head Office
Would not see my face again
Unless I became my own Scipio Africanus . . .
Dreamt of three headless crows
Flying in a room
Whose walls were silently burning.
Bald, toothless faces
Stood at a window, laughing in the rain,
Clapping to a fiddle's music —
Their naked, hairless bodies
The colour of sour milk.

Narwhal

Hedges of pack-ice
Line the forest where it grazes
On thorns of cuttle-fish.

Auroras of sheet-light
Spray it with arrows
Alongside paddocks of snow and moss.

Whistling and bellowing to itself,
It wanders through towers
Of glaciers, trumpeting:
A herald to days without beginnings or end.

Tapestries of lichen
Growing black and green, are a scrollwork
It never ceases to weave —
Diving over palisades of light
To straits and channels of pasture.

Harpooned or shot,
A legend dies in the Middle Ages —
Unicorns vanish on matted floes
Through squalls of mist that equators draw.

A scape-goat of reason
It roams in tribes
Over Arctic shelves and ridges,
Thrusting an ivory blade
At wings of sunlight that follow like a hawk.

Terminus

The first word is a spike
Against my forehead, a raised sledgehammer
Suspended in air.

The hallway surrounds me
With echoes. Bricks are witnesses
To the morning's betrayal.

Magpies hang their songs on the trees.
This Sunday is not an important Friday.

Should I have killed
What my heart was guessing at —
Saved eighty cents
And stayed in bed?

The world was ending in my dream
Until a blue and yellow bird flew down to my hand.
My room filling with water —
The bird refusing to fly away.

This morning's Christ is waiting at Mass,
Waiting in the coldness
You've been breathing through.
You carry the cross that's been built
By many — wiping your face
On every shred of prescribed advice.

One morning in church
The fear of death hit me head-on
Like a smash. I rushed out —
Still hearing the communion song
As I pumped the accelerator
Down the hill!

There isn't even time
To tell my dream. Perhaps you'd made sense
Out of what I'll live through?
I try to rationalize your own confessions.
Love is a dream we'll never interpret.

Calvary's the star we were both born under
And going to Mass the interim cure
For eternity's star-pocked headache:
The faith we live by,
And now surely die at.

The pips of "time up"
Jump four hundred miles like a rejoined nerve.
Goodbye is a word I've never understood.
For everything these three minutes have meant
I may as well have rung from hell.

I hang up the receiver
And the sledge hits home.

Hypochondriac

My little bottles
Stare back at me —
Open-mouthed, speechless,
Like bloated tropical fish.
Their contents gleam
With a luckystone polish.

Wads of cotton wool
Float like clouds —
Heaps of summer light
To fill my lungs with.
The doctor laughs, asks: "what for?"
I stuff my ears with it
And dare winds to enter uninvited.

Left on my palm
Their colours stain
Like boiled lollies —
Reds, blue, pollen yellow;
The gelatine dissolves in sweat.
Others you couldn't split
With a blade.

Some look like torpedoes,
Some balloons — are stamped
With letters or a sign.

One is tasteless,
Clear as glass or rain —
Shaped like a crystal ball
It crushes the easiest.

Migrant hostel

Parkes, 1949-51

No one kept count
Of all the comings and goings —
Arrivals of newcomers
In busloads from the station,
Sudden departures from adjoining blocks
That left us wondering
Who would be coming next.

Nationalities sought
Each other out instinctively —
Like a homing pigeon
Circling to get its bearings;
Years and place-names
Recognised by accents,
Partitioned off at night
By memories of hunger and hate.

For over two years
We lived like birds of passage —
Always sensing a change
In the weather:
Unaware of the season
Whose track we would follow.

A barrier at the main gate
Sealed off the highway
From our doorstep —
As it rose and fell like a finger
Pointed in reprimand or shame;
And daily we passed
Underneath or alongside it —
Needing its sanction
To pass in and out of lives
That had only begun
Or were dying.

Visiting hour

Tongues motionless
We bring flowers like gifts
Of seaweed washed up in nightmare squalls.

Each corridor
A white-tiled canyon —
Entrances to pillowed caves and wardrobe spiders
Where foxes scream in sulphur dust-storms.

A clockchime shatters
Our heartbeat and yours;
The moment of meeting is Lazarus dead twice:
Is a desert of blankets strewn
With fish-bone grass
Across your staring, river-drained face.

What can I say?
The hour nearly gone.
A glass of oranges left from morning
Is juice run sour through slates of light —
Sunflower reflections on the half-lit doorway
Over which you could not step.

A million years of nerve-growth
I crushed on to the accelerator, tonight.
Telling myself all the way in
These things must happen to you and us.

Arguing logic with myself
And the wind around the car's tyres —
A dummy clown, tarred and feathered,
Your psyche guardian from heaven:
Juggling cups of pain like acid bombs.

When hospitals were matchboxes
Found in gutters, pieced and glued together;
And lifts were apple trees we climbed with dogs,
You carried me through a host
Of leaves,
                    and autumn was a brown book
I could not keep away from.

Now I cram a thousand words
Into an hour of pages written for you —
Listening to the screams of foxes
In corridors you've been sweeping
Since the moment of my birth.

Chronic ward

After Ken Kesey's *One Flew Over the Cuckoo's Nest*

Mostly we talk about
The past and how we got here —
Where one's born
And why people must die in beds,
How the grass never wears out
With all the short cuts
The moon takes across our eyes
In waking and sleep.

At the state's expense
Or our mercy's appeasement —
Two, three, six or ten times a stay
We enact the mirror scene
For doctor, visitor and each other:
Relive the bathtub drama,
The slip-knot confusion
And oven-door mistakes
Before breakfast, lunch or dinner.

Sometimes one of us
Makes it — sees Buddha
Or Jesus Christ
Under their respective, flowering trees
And reports to the others:
All's well with angels; and hell's
Not so frightening either —
Speaks on the reliability
Of x-rays, lumbar punctures
And lobotomized skulls.

We tread the carpet
Of our shadows' patterns
Like playing a game of stepping on cracks—
Day and night, as we talk ourselves into sleep:
Every time someone falters,
Slips or dies in mid-air
We count to ten before taking a breath—
Our voices catching up with us

Somewhere between
The night's waking and tomorrow's other death.

Discharged

Home at last
You're still the stranger
I couldn't recognise
Without a word being spoken first.

The dog jumps
Like a wound-up Jack-in-the box.
Smiling in whispers
You stoop to pat him.

I was wrong—
Your eyes didn't turn blue
From the *Celestone*
They used to cure you.

Where do
We all go from here?
There've been no corridors
Added in your absence.

The garden weeded,
Washing all done — Father
Managed to survive the week
On a pound of steak
And the vegetables you left him.
The milkman kept on
Leaving bottles.

Moving from
Room to room — touching
A table, lounge suite, curtains,
A saucer that's older
Than all of us put together,
You become a part of the house
We thought had died.

My book-cases
That you covered with sheets
Like snowdrift shrouds
Creak on the floor
At the door's opening.

What more can
We do, right now?
In your stockinged feet
We don't even know what room
You're heading for?

Father and I
Look at each other
Across the kitchen sink.
A bedroom door opens.
You still haven't said a word.

Still-born

How cold
Was the darkness
That shrouded you —
Left you in silence
Before silence was known,
Closed your eyes
And bowed your head,
Dove-like, unmoving?

How gentle
Were the hands
That brought you into light —
Held you from
Expected promises,
Turning you swiftly
Away from your mother?

How loud
Was the cry
You never heard —
That tore from the shallows of bone
Like a fish, desperate,
Half-dead for air?

How long
Were the dreams
That preceded your coming?
Nights of waking
And burnt-out patience
You will never know?

Where will
They go to — the man
And woman that lay claim to you,
Speaking the name
By which you will be known?

Flower garden

1

My parents' garden
Always seemed
Too full of flowers!
Gardenias, cyclamens, irises,
Jasmine, carnations
And roses — a host
Of royal names
I could never remember.

Visitors came
And left with bouquets
To shoulder-height —
Like pilgrims setting out
For a street
Of wayside shrines.

Eventually
The upkeep grew into
A burden:
Three-quarters of the garden
Uprooted, burned,
The ashes thrown into
Duck Creek.

2

Back from school
I'd sit cross-legged
Among the rows,
My blue cap lost
In a maze of colour —
Catching ants, dropping caterpillars
Into half-open buds,
Teasing bees
With a flicking handkerchief.

3

Promising
Not to pick flowers
I left briskly
For school in the mornings —
A spring-and-summer madness
That nobody
Ever explained,
A snapdragon
In my left-hand coat pocket:
The talisman
I wouldn't part with
Until it withered
Into red or purple dust

4

I said nothing
When the garden lost
Its flowers —
Time wielding a scythe
In whose path
We had to follow.
The snapdragons
Were first to go.

Asylum

Eyes never open
In this house without walls.

Behind every closed door
A head reclines
On a pillow of darkness.

Steps are granite
Worn smooth by winds — the shifting
Of weight from mind to feet.

Trees and hedges
Crowd the windows: ghost-gums,
Thistle, shades of palm.
No one looks out.

Shadows flutter like
Trapped birds. Webs of moonlight
Hang from a ceiling.

Stars are flowers on faces of chalk,
Pock-marked by rain, studded with hail.

In daylight it is not there,
Clouds hanging over
Like a bushfire. Roadways
Lead into mountains or rivers.

At night you cannot escape it.
Like sleep on death's
Threshold, it confronts you:
Eyes believing only what they cannot see.

Waking is a reminder
Of winds crying in hallways
That were never built —
Dreams you can sometimes remember.

Hands at morning tap on doors,
Wiping the breath of mists from a window —
Coming in like supplicants,
Without a meaning to your dream.

Heritage

There will always be
A face that you never see —
That falls into shadow
At every sunset.

A hundred fingers
Will always point at you
From the mirror
In a drop of rain.

You will stir
The depths of every pool
You find — drop pebbles,
Pull out weeds.

Trying to pray
You will imagine God beside you
On the raw earth
Of a dug grave.

There will be
No God — devil, father or mother
Looking back
From the bottom of a pool.

Not even among
Poisoned roots and grassblades
Will the splash of rain
Grow louder or faint.

The eyes of your child
Remind you of water and stone —
It is the answer to a question
That no one will ever ask.

Appointment: north-west

At Jeogla I heard
The mountains tremble,
Saw trees shed their leaves
As a storm approached:
Heard the wind speak out
From under stones,
Watching clouds hang motionless
Over dogs and cattle.

It was the country
Of frosts and rain, bleak drizzles
That turned walls damp.
Rainbows grew
From the pond in our garden —
Covered the Big Hill
In a waterfall of mist.

In summer the hills
Ran green with sheep, willows
Along creeks
And riderless horses.

Winter turned
A blind eye to hands,
Left its cracks on lips
And knuckles.
At first you checked thermometers
Regularly, like a heartbeat —
Then learnt about weather
From the colours of a tree.

There you become
The movement of silences,
Listen to yourself
Talking to magpies and crows —
Spend whole afternoons
Sitting on the edge of a dam
Watching the faces
Of dragonflies and geese.

Through drifts
Of evening snow
Voices call from gullies.
A gate or fence-post answers back.
Dreams crackle in chimneys
Blacker than night.

People turn towards
The hills for words — hunt kangaroos
To show visitors
They don't stay home at night:
Withdraw to themselves,
Talking of dingo baits —
How tanks and pipes
Stand up to the cold.

Deserted houses
Crowd stones on the track
Of a closed-down school and sawmill.
Blackberry bushes
Hide lizards and snakes
That watch from
Roofs of rusted sheet-iron.

There you look
For early sunsets —
An on-coming trail of dust
Along the road,
A stranger or friend that passes.
Your own voice listening
To the whisper of leaves —
As though a mother or father
Was speaking to caution.

Leaving each time
Was a promise to return,
To settle among hills
That could hide you forever —
Knowing time was a crow
You'd never snare,
Or the axe that wouldn't rust
In its block on the woodheap.

In the folk museum

A darkness in the rooms
Betrays the absence of voices,
Departing from steps
And veranda rails –
On to a street that leads around Autumn
Which stands at the door
Dressed in yellow and brown.

I look at words
That describe machinery, clothes, transport,
A Victorian Bedroom –
Hay knife, draining plough,
Shoulder yoke, box iron:
Relics from a Tablelands heritage
To remind me of a past
Which isn't mine.

The caretaker sits
Beside a winnowing machine
And knits without looking up –
Her hair's the same colour
As the grey clay bottle
That's cold as water to touch.

In the Town Hall next door
They sing to Christ –
Of the Sabbath Day and the Future of Man.
I try to memorize
The titles of books
While "Eternity, Eternity"
Is repeated from a reader's text.

The wind taps hurriedly
On the roof and walls
And I leave without wanting a final look.
At the door the old woman's hand
Touches mine.
"Would you please sign the Visitors' Book?"

On Barren Hill

1

We pick the hips
Off briar roses that straggle
Over fences —
While black mosquitoes
Sting our necks
And magpies hurl
Their glances.

The city wakes
Below us
On a yellowing autumn morning —
Like the bark
On dying trees
Our words
Hang upon its air.

"There's St Mary's,
And St Peter's — the pines
In Central Park.

"There's the place
You're staying at —
And here
The road we came up."

2

Pockets filled,
Curiosity satisfied, sheep scatter
At our descent —

Puff-balls
Floating across the track
Catch
      on the thorns

Of briar roses.

A drive in the country

At Blue Hole
I stood by the water's edge
And watched how swallows swam
Through the air —
Wild ducks moving away
In the weeds
To their nests in the hollows
Of blackberries and reeds.

I stood on a rock
By the roots of a willow —
Saw how leaves
Bent their ears to the ground.
Gum trees shed
Their bark to the wind
And she-oaks dipped their hands
In the shallows.

A chain and rope
Hung down from a tree —
Over the water for children to swing from.
And I thought of a gallows
To which dead men return
At noon or in darkness
To wait for a crowd.

And still I kept looking
Back to the road —
Away from Blue Hole
And the miles yet to go:
Thinking of the room
Where an alarm clock was set
And tomorrow already there.

But only the soft call
Of swallows and wild ducks
Replied to my thoughts
Through the streamers
Of blue light.

I spoke to myself
Like a man who is dying
And walks away from a road
That runs only one way.

Famous novelist

He tells me
Life's a question mark poised
Like a snake
In his dreams —
"You take hold of the end
Nearest you
And be drawn into oceans of sleep.

"Morning's a shoreline
Of flotsam,
Razor-lines of light across open eyes —
The imprints of an invisible
Goddess
Who crushes Ego at will."
Flowers gleam by a doorstep.
Leaves rustle in a conversation of their own.

In half-light
I stare
At eyes like jaded pearl
In which discs
Of ebony spin.
"Character is a nerve end,"
He pauses,
"Exposed to the scalpels of Fortune
And its own
Indecisive whims."
Night presses closer and listens.
The gutter runs silver at our feet.

The meeting's
Cursory, a moment's whipcrack
On Time's unravelling skein —
"Fame is a two-way
Mirror,"
He concludes,
"In which a death's-head
Perpetually grins."

The night air smothers
Our parting words
Like green grass thrown on to flames.
A car's tyres
Scream in the distance.
The cold sweat of a handshake remains.

The music net

The cold whisper of rain
Creeps into
The conversation
Like a shadow on our backs —
Pauses, by an unsigned portrait
Of a staring, red-eyed girl —
Inarticulate, alone.

Now, at the piano
She declares: "Rachmaninov had a preoccupation
With Russian bells,"
And the voice of a Prelude rises
From a terrace house
Whose walls surround us like
Stacked bones.

And I think of water washing
Over stones
That must sink and die
In the earth —
Sustained by air, salt or rain
Till lightning snaps their throats
Like human nerves
And they cry out
In a song of anguished praise.

The music fades
With the rain and silence
Draws us from the room together.
At the door she glances
At her portrait, asks: "Shall we go elsewhere
And listen to Mahler?"

Memorial grove

Morning flutes the air
Through reeds and night's rain hangs
In a crown of trees —
Finches scatter from a hawthorn
Like stones flung skywards
To distract a thief.
Bulbul, silvereye, dove, drink
At the pond's edge.

In the centre, toppled,
Its wiring twisted, stonework cracked —
Barely touching water,
A vase-shaped monument with
A grey inscription:
Christ. The Fountain Of Living Waters.
A pair of green frogs croak
On a lily-pad's back.

Around me the silence
Of cemetery and suburbs comes down
Like a canopy of eyes:
Unspeaking, watchful,
Resenting the intrusion of curiosity —
While memory stares
At a phrase
That confounds the interpretation
Of logic.

I stand on a track
Nearly a hundred years old
And remember the king
Who turned Water into Gold.

Fiddler crabs

Scuttling across
Marshlands or sandy flats
In search of food
They live between the change of tides —
In colours that separate
Day from night.

At sunrise
Their shells darken,
Grow stronger, become coarse —
Like charcoal or lava
On which spores
Could never take root.

At evening
The darkness dissolves —
Small star-shapes
Are patterned in greens and yellow
That leave the shell
A polished mosaic.

Camouflaged from themselves
They return through
Mud and salt to their burrows
Hastily — as if
Running away with a secret:
A dome of sunlight
That humans aren't meant to see
Ingrown on their backs
Like a cross for eternity.

Widowed

Hardly a day passes
That she doesn't work
In her garden — pruning and weeding
On bended knees,
Watching the dance of bees
In clumps of lantana
Overgrowing her paths.

She pauses longest
Among the roses — fingering
Petals and buds
As if they were the hem
Of a wedding or christening dress —
Shyly, almost reluctant.

Again and again
She returns to a hedge
Or vine — stands
As though waiting
For something to happen.

Kneeling on leaves
She won't burn,
On decayed rain
That has turned to moss,
She tends to violets and marigolds —
Her dress gathered about her
Like a garment of ceremony:
Her face overshadowed
By a hat which summer can't pierce,
Her future entangled
Among thorns and evergreens.

Outside the delivery room

They have given me
A green coat
That ties up at the back —
Straightjacket and bib
In which to dress my emotions —
My footsteps
Clattering up the stairs
Because I wouldn't
Wait for the lift.

The telephone message
Still crackles
In my head — every inch
Of five or six miles;
The doctor's voice
Imbued with a calmness
That makes me
Think of ether
And bright lights.

I didn't even
Stop to buy flowers —
Card or fruit
To decorate my hands.
Thrilled and
Afraid, I raced
April's weather along
The highway — imagining
I was a piece of paper
Blown by chance
Into the hospital grounds.

What shall
I say — "Well done"
Or speak of love?
Make promises?
The nurse tells me
I can go in.
Hurriedly, I stretch
Out my arms,
Push open the swinging doors —
As if I suddenly
Realized where I was
And had to find
                    my way
Out of a labyrinth.

Kornelia Woloszczuk

Her face
Betrays the darkness of storms,
Winds that alter
The outline of a coast —
Eyes to outstare
The face of the waters:
As if hands
Were dragging
The depths of a swamp
In search
Of her lost son.

Being
Her only child,
Where did I go wrong?
Not knowing
The cave of silence
In which
She outwaited
Tides of absence, seas
Of loneliness
That lapped her dress
Like a prayerwheel,
Confined to the centre
Of a wasteland
On her palms?

In springtime
She walks beside
A river, pointing out
How water destroys images
That reflect eternity:
Grassblades, leaves, flowers —
At whose roots
A fire burns
When a man forsakes
His wife and child.
Her feet
Make no imprint
Upon the grass
She treads.

Walking
Behind her
I listen for birdcalls,
Look at breaking water
With every fish in air —
Nervous, uncertain
Of distances and colours
We pass through.
A dream, she says,
Is the path from God:
A faith to cherish
What you inherit
At birth — sustain the winds
On which prophets spoke
Across seas
And ruins of hills.
All is sacrificed
For the sake of children
Who forget you
Before you are dead —

But, remember,
"Having only one child
Is like having
One eye in your head."

Post card

1

A post card sent by a friend
Haunts me
Since its arrival —
Warsaw: Panorama of the Old Town.
He requests I show it
To my parents.

Red buses on a bridge
Emerging from a corner —
High-rise flats and something
Like a park borders
The river with its concrete pylons.
The sky's the brightest shade.

2

Warsaw, Old Town,
I never knew you
Except in the third person —
Great city
That bombs destroyed,
Its people massacred
Or exiled — You survived
In the minds
Of a dying generation
Half a world away.
They shelter you
And defend the patterns
Of your remaking,
Condemn your politics,
Cherish your old religion
And drink to freedom
Under the White Eagle's flag.

For the moment,
I repeat, I never knew you,
Let me be.
I've seen red buses
Elsewhere
And all rivers have
An obstinate glare.
My father
Will be proud
Of your domes and towers,
My mother
Will speak of her
Beloved Ukraine.
What's my choice
To be?

I can give you
The recognition
Of eyesight and praise.
What more
Do you want
Besides
The gift of despair?

3

I stare
At the photograph
And refuse to answer
The voices
Of red gables
And a cloudless sky.

On the river's bank
A lone tree
Whispers:
"We will meet
Before you die."

Add to your poetry collection with UQP's acclaimed series

OLD/NEW WORLD Peter Skrzynecki
978 0 7022 3586 3

'*Old/New World* is a fitting tribute to a poet who … uses Wordsworthian lyricism to convey migrant experience to telling effect.' *Australian Book Review*

TWO KINDS OF SILENCE Kathryn Lomer
978 0 7022 3612 9
Winner 2008 NSW Premier's Literary Awards – The Kenneth Slessor Poetry Prize

'This is a book which shows the breadth of Lomer's range and also her facility for subtle nuanced language.' *Sunday Tasmanian*

PARTS OF SPEECH Angela Gardner
978 0 7022 3615 0
Winner 2006 Thomas Shapcott Award

'Angela Gardner's *Parts of Speech* shows what a substantial first book of poetry is all about.' *Cordite Poetry Review*

REVOLVING DAYS: SELECTED POEMS David Malouf
978 0 7022 3635 8
Winner 2008 Queensland Premier's Literary Awards – Arts Queensland Judith Wright Calanthe Award for a Poetry Collection

'*Revolving Days* is a masterwork from one of our greatest poets.' *Sydney Morning Herald*

BARK Anthony Lawrence
978 0 7022 3664 8

'Polished, intellectually nimble, punctuated by moments of superb description, they are evidence of a vigorous talent.' *Sydney Morning Herald*

THE BALCONY David Brooks
978 0 7022 3669 3

'Brooks commands a poetic style that is energetic, exacting, but also happy to be plain.' *Canberra Times*

ARIA Sarah Holland-Batt
978 0 7022 3675 4
Winner 2007 Thomas Shapcott Award
Winner 2009 FAW Anne Elder Award for a First Book of Poetry
Winner 2009 ACT Poetry Prize – The Judith Wright Prize

'*Aria* is a most haunting and impressive debut volume.' *Sydney Morning Herald*

DIVINE COMEDY: JOURNEYS THROUGH A REGIONAL GEOGRAPHY
John Kinsella
978 0 7022 3666 2

'Kinsella's version of that poem reveals that here he is at the full stretch of his powers, with a subject and setting at once universal and particular to engage, with a moral passion that infuses all that he attempts to depict, and a craft fit for such a grand enterprise.' *Canberra Times*

APPLES WITH HUMAN SKIN Nathan Shepherdson
978 0 7022 3741 6

'*Apples with Human Skin* is the work of an experienced and skilled poet, and the images are both compelling and beautifully honed.' *Australian Book Review*

VANISHING POINT Felicity Plunkett
978 0 7022 3721 8
Winner 2008 Thomas Shapcott Award

'A dynamic collection dealing with life's big issues marks the emergence of a major new talent.' *Sydney Morning Herald*

PARTS OF US Thomas Shapcott
978 0 7022 3769 0

'*Parts of Us* is witty, clever and thought-provoking. It is also deeply moving, a powerful testament to a life and an art.' *Sydney Morning Herald*

AN ABSENCE OF SAINTS Rosanna Licari
978 0 7022 3843 7

'Licari has a magical ability to respond to – and then express – the essential strangeness, not only of objects and places but of our experience of life itself.' Martin Duwell

STARLIGHT: 150 POEMS John Tranter
978 0 7022 3845 1

'An intensity, and a many-sided explorativeness [unmatched] in Australian poetry.' Martin Duwell